Contents

Some words are shown in bold, **like this**. They are explained in "Words to know" on page 23.

Plants

Plants are living things. Plants need water to grow. Plants need air to grow. Plants need sunlight to grow. Plants need **nutrients** to grow.

Spot the Difference

Plants

CUSTOMER SERVICE EXCELLENCE

Libraries & Archives

ebecca Rissman

www.raintreepublishers.co.uk
Visit our website to find out more information about Raintree books.

To order:
☎ Phone 0845 6044371
▤ Fax +44 (0) 1865 312263
▣ Email myorders@capstonepub.co.uk

Customers from outside the UK please telephone +44 1865 312262

Raintree is an imprint of Capstone Global Library Limited, a company incorporated in England and Wales having its registered office at 7 Pilgrim Street, London, EC4V 6LB – Registered company number: 6695582

Text © Capstone Global Library Limited 2009
First published in hardback in 2009
Paperback edition first published in 2010
The moral rights of the proprietor have been asserted.

Edited by Rebecca Rissman, Siân Smith, and Charlotte Guillain
Designed by Kimberly Miracle and Joanna Malivoire
Picture research by Elizabeth Alexander
Originated by Heinemann Library
Printed in China by Leo Paper Group

ISBN 978 0 431194 17 2 (hardback)
13 12 11 10 09
10 9 8 7 6 5 4 3 2 1

ISBN 978 0 431194 22 6 (paperback)
14 13 12 11 10
10 9 8 7 6 5 4 3 2 1

British Library Cataloguing in Publication Data
Rissman, Rebecca
Plants. - (Can you spot the difference?) (Acorn plus)
1. Plants - Variation - Pictorial works - Juvenile literature
I. Title
581

Acknowledgments
The author and publishers are grateful to the following for permission to reproduce copyright material: Alamy pp. **6**, **7** (© Phil Degginger), **10** (© Caro), **13 left** (© Klaus-Peter Wolf), **15 left** (© M.Brodie), **22 bottom left** (© K-Pix), **22 bottom right** (© Oleksiy Maksymenko); Corbis pp. **4** (© Visuals Unlimited), **5 left** (© LWA- JDC), **11 right** (© Frans Lanting), **17 left** (© Hal Horwitz), **18** (© Dave Michaels), **19 right** (© J.C.Valette/ photocuisine); Getty Images pp. **14** (Heinz Wohner/LOOK), **20** (Jeffrey Conley/Photonica); Photolibrary pp. **5 right** (Santokh Kochar/Photodisc), **9 left** (Photodisc/Glen Allison), **9 right** (Boone Jessica/Botanica), **12** (Animals Animals/ Richard Shiell), **13 right** (Bill Schildge/Pacific Stock), **16** (Kerstin Layer/Mauritius), **21** (Astra Production/Picture Press), **22 top left** (Adalberto Rios Szalay/Sexto Sol/Photodisc), **22 top right** (Botanica); Punchstock p. **8** (Photodisc); Shutterstock pp. **11 left** (© Muriel Lasure), **15 right** (© Gordana Sermek), **17 right** (© Tihis), **19 left** (© Arne Sieglin).

Cover photograph reproduced with permission of Shutterstock (© Gautier Willaume). Back cover photograph reproduced with permission of Shutterstock (© Gordana Sermek).

We would like to thank Nancy Harris and Adriana Scalise for their help in the preparation of this book.

Every effort has been made to contact copyright holders of any material reproduced in this book. Any omissions will be rectified in subsequent printings if notice is given to the publisher.

Plants grow in many places. Some plants grow in **soil**. Some plants grow in water.

Plant parts

Plants have many parts. Each part helps the plant in a different way.

flower

leaf

stem

roots

Roots

Most plants have **roots**. Roots bring water into the plant. Roots help plants to stay in place.

There are many types of roots. Some roots are big and long. Some roots are short and round.

Stems

Most plants have **stems**. Stems hold **leaves** and **flowers** up. Stems bring water to leaves and flowers.

There are many types of stem. Some stems are thick. Some stems are thin. Some stems are curly.

Leaves

Most plants have **leaves**. Leaves use sunlight to make food for the plant. Plants need food to help them grow.

There are many types of leaves. Some leaves are very big. Some leaves are long and thin.

Flowers

Some plants have **flowers**. Flowers make **seeds** that grow into new plants.

There are many types of flowers. Some flowers are very small. Some flowers are many different colours.

Fruits

Many plants grow **fruits**. Fruits have **seeds** in them.
Seeds grow into new plants.

Most fruits have smooth skin on the outside, but some fruits do not. Thorn apple fruits have spiky skin. Kiwi fruits have furry skin.

Seeds

Plants grow from **seeds**. Seeds **travel** to new places in different ways. Some seeds are blown in the wind or float in water. Insects and other animals help seeds travel, too.

seeds

Some plants grow many seeds. Some plants grow a few seeds or only one seed.

What do plants do?

People and other animals need to breathe in **oxygen** from the air. Plants give out the oxygen we need.

Plants make their own food. Plants can be food for people and other animals, too!

Spot the difference!

How many differences can you see?

Words to know

flower part of a plant that makes seeds

fruit part of a plant that holds seeds

leaf part of a plant that uses sunlight to make food

nutrient something in the soil that helps plants to grow healthily

oxygen one of the gases in the air. Humans and other animals need to breathe in oxygen to stay alive.

roots part of a plant that can hold it in the ground. Roots bring water to the plant.

seed something that can grow into a new plant. Plants make seeds.

soil the top part of the ground. Many plants need to grow in soil.

stem part of a plant that holds the plant up. Stems also carry water to different parts of the plant.

travel to move from place to place

Index

Notes for parents and teachers

Before reading

Discuss with children that plants are living things and that they need air, sunlight, water, and nutrients to grow. Show children a picture of a plant and provide the following labels: "roots," "stem," "seeds," "flower," and "leaves." Ask the children to put the labels where they think they should go on the picture. Discuss their choices.

On page 17

Talk about the fact that it is dangerous to eat fruits without knowing what they are. Discuss the difference between fruits we can eat and poisonous fruits which could make us ill or die if we eat them. On p.17 both the kiwi fruit and the thorn apple can be eaten, but the thorn apple can be poisonous if the fruit is unripe.

After reading

• Take children on a nature walk. Point out different types of plants and ask children what they see. Are there leaves on the plant? Stems? Flowers?

• Bring in a variety of leaves. Ask children which ways they can sort the leaves (e.g. by colour, shape, roughness, or smoothness). Split children into four groups. Ask each group to sort a pile of leaves, then to share and explain the categories they chose for the leaves.

• Help children to plant broad bean seeds individually or plant one bean seed as a whole class activity. Soak the beans in water overnight and plant them into clear plastic cups the following day. Discuss the parts of the plant as the plant grows. Children can keep a journal of drawings to show what they see each day.